W9-BNS-091

IS THE
SAXOPHONE
FOR YOU?

ELAINE LANDAU

Lerner Publications Company · Minneapolis

Lerner Publications Company
A division of Lerner Publishing Group, Inc.
241 First Avenue North
Minneapolis, MN 55401 U.S.A.

Website address: www.lernerbooks.com

Library of Congress Cataloguing-in-Publication Data

Landau, Elaine.
    Is the saxophone for you? / by Elaine Landau.
        p.   cm. — (Ready to make music)
    Includes bibliographical references and index.
    ISBN: 978-0-7613-5425-3 (lib. bdg. : alk. paper)
    1. Saxophone—Juvenile literature. I. Title.
ML975.L36 2011
788.7'19—dc22   2009048969

Manufactured in the United States of America
1 – DP – 7/15/10

CONTENTS

CHAPTER ONE

BIG, BOLD, AND BRASSY

Picture this:

You play the saxophone with a well-known jazz trio. It's the last night of the group's very successful tour. You're playing to a sold-out crowd in Washington, D.C. A lot of important people are in the audience tonight. The president of the United States and the First Lady may even be among them.

You go onstage determined to give your all. Your dazzling solo brings the audience to its feet. You've worked hard for years to be as good as you are. Tonight it paid off. You shined as brightly as a star.

This saxophonist plays a solo to show off his skills.

This jazz trio features *(from left to right)* a double bass, a saxophone, and a piano.

Then switch to this scene. You're a saxophone player with a famous rock band. Tonight's show is special for you. You're playing in your hometown. Your parents, former principal, and music teacher are part of the crowd.

You've got nothing to worry about, though. The power and passion of your wailing sax drive the audience wild. The next day, the local papers rave about you. Life doesn't get any better than this.

Can you see yourself in one of these scenes? The saxophone can be used to play many types of music. So with enough hard work and dedication, you might be either one of these musicians someday.

MEET THE WOODWINDS— WHAT A LOVELY FAMILY!

You come from a family. You may look or sound a lot like your family members. Do you have your father's laugh? Your mother's curly hair? And hey—are those your aunt Birdie's dimples?

Instruments are grouped into families too. The saxophone is in the woodwind family. Wait! That doesn't sound right. Saxophones are made of brass. Aren't instruments in the woodwind family made of wood?

Many woodwind instruments are wooden, but not all. So then what do woodwind instruments have in common? All of them are played by blowing air either over or through them. Woodwinds such as the sax also use a small piece of wood called a reed to make noise. When a musician blows air into the mouthpiece, the reed vibrates (moves back and forth). This creates the sound we hear. Other popular members of the woodwind family include the flute, the clarinet, and the bassoon.

6

The flute isn't usually made out of wood, but it is a woodwind.

The saxophone is a great instrument. People like the look of this large, bright, shiny horn. When they hear a sax, many fall in love with its smooth, rich sound. It's easy to become a saxophone fan. What makes the saxophone so special? Here's just the short list.

FEELING THE MUSIC

Sax players love their instruments. They use the saxophone to express their feelings. "The sax is a very special instrument because of the emotions it can deliver," says saxophonist James Hayward. "It can show exactly how I feel when I'm playing. If I am playing a happy piece of music, that emotion will come through. If it's a sad or moody song, that emotion will come out as well." That's quite an instrument! The saxophone lets you play music that shows your heart and soul.

The sax is a great instrument for expressing emotion.

If you enjoy some time in the spotlight, the saxophone could be a good fit for you.

KEEP IT COOL

When you think about sax players, do you imagine stylish sunglasses? What about carefree personalities? Lots of people think that the saxophone is one of the coolest instruments around. A sax player can set the mood at a concert or even steal the show. The saxophone is a great choice for people who like to stand out from the crowd.

MORE THAN ONE IS FUN

Think there's only one kind of saxophone? If so, think again. There are lots of different saxophones. Like people, this instrument comes in various shapes and sizes. So people of different sizes and ages can pick the sax that's right for them. Each saxophone plays a different range of notes as well. Let's hear a cheer for variety!

Just say the word *saxophone*. The tenor sax is what most people think of. The tenor sax has a curved mouthpiece and a bell (a wide end that flares out). It's a popular choice for jazz musicians.

The alto saxophone is a great choice for beginners. The alto and tenor saxophones look a lot alike, but the alto sax is smaller. An alto sax player doesn't need to blow as much air into his or her instrument to make a sound. Musicians who are just starting out won't have trouble making noise with an alto sax.

The alto sax is a good pick for beginning musicians.

Is that really a saxophone? That's what you might say after seeing a soprano sax for the first time. This sax looks more like a clarinet than a tenor or alto sax. It's a straight tube that flares into a bell at one end. The soprano sax is the smallest saxophone. It also produces the highest notes.

A few different types of saxes are (from left to right) soprano, alto, tenor, and baritone.

Saxophonists James Rivers and Donald Harrison Jr. jam with other musicians at the New Orleans Jazz and Heritage Festival in 2006.

The baritone sax is called the bari for short. The bari is not as widely used as the alto and tenor saxophones. But you'd notice it if you saw it. The baritone sax is large and heavy. Baritone saxophones weigh between 15 and 20 pounds (6.8 to 9 kilograms)! Bari players sometimes wear a special harness to support the instrument.

Lots of sax players play more than one type of saxophone. They may not have a favorite. They love all the warm sounds a saxophone can make.

THE PARTS OF THE ALTO SAXOPHONE

You learn about the different parts of your body at school. It's important to take good care of each of these parts. You've got to take good care of your saxophone too. So you'll want to know all about its parts. Are you ready? We're about to begin a tour of the sax.

BELL

The bell is the end part of the saxophone. It flares out into a bell shape. Sounds leave the saxophone here.

TUBE

The tube is the straight part of the saxophone's body. Air passes through the tube on its way to the sax's bell.

BOW

The bow is the U-shaped bottom of the saxophone's body.

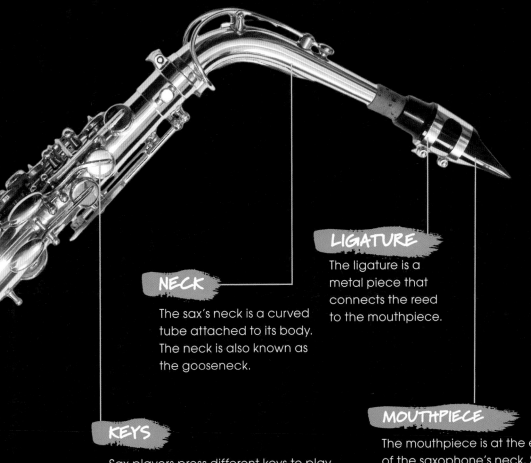

NECK

The sax's neck is a curved tube attached to its body. The neck is also known as the gooseneck.

LIGATURE

The ligature is a metal piece that connects the reed to the mouthpiece.

KEYS

Sax players press different keys to play different notes. Pressing down the keys lifts the pads. The sax lets out a higher note.

MOUTHPIECE

The mouthpiece is at the end of the saxophone's neck. Sax players puts their lips on the mouthpiece and blow air into the instrument. The sax's reed attaches to the mouthpiece.

THUMB REST

The thumb rest is a hook-shaped part where a sax player places his or her right thumb to support the weight of the instrument.

CHAPTER TWO

SO MANY WAYS TO PLAY

Music is everywhere. It's part of all our lives. You might hear music in an elevator, in the grocery store, or while riding the bus. Listen for a saxophone the next time you hear a song. The sax pops up in all kinds of music.

ROCK AND ROLL

What if you love the sax but only want to play rock music? Do those two things go together? You bet they do! The sax has found its place in the world of rock.

Have you ever heard of the group Morphine? Morphine was a rock group without a guitar. The sax was its lead instrument. Singer Mark Sandman and sax player Dana Colley formed Morphine in 1990. Colley played both tenor and baritone sax. People said that Colley played the sax as if it were a guitar. He was compared to guitar legend Jimi Hendrix.

14

Dana Colley rocks out at the South by Southwest Music Festival in 1994 in Austin, Texas.

Sadly, this group ended too soon. In 1999 Sandman passed away after a heart attack at the age of forty-seven. But in 2009, Colley formed a new group with drummer Jerome Deupree. They began playing Morphine songs as well as new material. Colley keeps proving that the sax has a place in rock.

ABI HARDING

Abi Harding is a sax player who rocks! Harding adds energy to the music of the British rock band the Zutons. Her fiery saxophone playing helps the band stand out from the crowd. Harding first went onstage for a performance with the Zutons in 2002. The band liked her style so much that she has been with them ever since. Are you a fan of both the sax and rock and roll? Then check out the Zutons. You just may love what you hear!

Abi Harding at the Coachella Valley Music and Arts Festival in 2006 in Indio, California

Want to hear the sax really soar? Listen to Bruce Springsteen and the E Street Band. Saxophone player Clarence "The Big Man" Clemons pumps life into the E Street Band's music. Don't miss Clemons's famous sax solos on the album *Born to Run*. Springsteen and the E Street Band have stayed popular since the 1970s. The Big Man's rocking sax is a big reason why.

Clarence Clemons *(left)* plays powerful sax music while Bruce Springsteen plays the guitar.

THE SAX AND JAZZ—
WHAT A COMBO!

Are you a jazz fan who loves the saxophone? What a match! People say the saxophone is the perfect instrument for jazz. You'll have to decide if that combo is perfect for you.

Jazz is less structured than many other types of music. Musicians often make up their music as they play it. This is known as improvisation. It allows the musician's feelings to come through. Sax players speak to the audience through their instrument this way.

There are many wonderful jazz saxophonists. Be sure to listen to the jazz greats of the past. No one should miss Charlie "Bird" Parker's music. Bird played alto sax like no one before him.

Parker was an important force in developing bebop jazz. Bebop is fast-moving dance music. Much of Charlie Parker's music was upbeat with a blues twist. He could make you feel both joy and sadness through his music. Some people say that Charlie Parker helped make the sax the voice of jazz.

Charlie Parker with his saxophone in 1947

LET'S PLAY THE LATIN WAY!

Have you ever heard merengue music? If not, it's only fair to warn you: When you hear it, you won't want to stay in your seat. It's hard not to move to this joyous sound.

Merengue is the name for a dance as well as a type of music. In the Dominican Republic, merengue is the national dance. Merengue dancing is popular in other parts of Latin America as well.

Are you a sax player who likes moving to merengue? You're in luck! Most modern merengue bands use saxophones. You may be playing this great music someday. If you do, one thing is certain: you and your listeners will have a lively time.

A sax player keeps the music of this Dominican Republic merengue band lively and fun.

John Coltrane is another jazz giant. This sax player was known for his lengthy improvisations. Coltrane's long solos were an important part of his sound. He said he used this time to explore the music. Many listeners say that Coltrane's album *Giant Steps* is a masterpiece. It's full of one-of-a-kind jazz songs.

CLASSICAL SAX

True or False:

You can like the sax and *not* like jazz or rock.

Hope you answered "true." Different people like different things. Maybe rock and jazz don't appeal to you. There's nothing wrong with preferring classical music.

John Coltrane had a unique talent for sax playing.

But most symphony orchestras do not regularly use saxophones. Don't let that discourage you, though. Some classical pieces do have parts for the sax.

Besides, you can also play classical music in music ensembles. These are small musical groups. Think about the fun you'd have playing with other woodwind wizards in a classical ensemble. Or jamming with other sax players in a saxophone quartet!

Sax players take part in a classical performance in Austria.

THE HISTORY OF THE SAXOPHONE

The saxophone is more than 150 years old. That may seem really old to you. But as far as musical instruments go, the sax is fairly young.

Adolphe Sax invented the saxophone in the early 1840s. Sax was an instrument maker and musician from Belgium who spent much of his life in Paris, France. He expected the instrument to be used by orchestras and concert bands. Sax never could have guessed where his instrument would end up. After the birth of jazz, jazz musicians claimed the sax as their own. By the 1920s, most jazz bands had a sax player. These days the sax is used in many types of music. Its sound is loved in countries around the world.

The year 1992 was big for the saxophone. Sax-playing politician Bill Clinton was elected president of the United States.

CHAPTER THREE

THE SAXOPHONE AND YOU

Does this describe you? You love music. You want it to be a big part of your life. You're pretty sure you'd like to play the sax. But is it the right choice for you? Let's look at some different reasons why musicians picked the saxophone.

Some sax players are inspired by musical relatives.

FAMILY INFLUENCE

Some musicians come from musical families. That's how sax player James Noyes got started.

"My father used to sing and play the banjo," Noyes recalled. "My mother was a singer who sang in the church choir. Both my sisters played instruments too.

When I was old enough, it was my turn to pick an instrument. I thought about playing the sax, the trumpet, or the drums. I passed on the trumpet. One of my sisters already played it. So I settled on the sax, and I'm glad I did."

In other cases, people choose an instrument that an older relative has played. That's George Garzone's story. "My uncle Rocco was a sax player," said Garzone. "When he died, he left his instrument to me. The saxophone became my instrument too."

A MOUNTAIN WOODWIND

The siku is a traditional instrument from the mountainous Andes region of South America. To create a siku, pipes made from bamboo shoots are bound together. The length of each pipe determines its pitch. To play the siku, a musician blows across the edge of a pipe. Musicians of many cultures have played the siku, so it goes by a few other names. People also call it the zampoña and the antara.

Children from the South American country of Bolivia play the zampoña.

Still other people choose to play an instrument precisely because no one else in their family does! Playing an instrument can help them to stand out. That's why Kermit Virgil started playing sax. "I was the youngest child in a large family," he explained. "I had seven brothers and sisters. None of them was musical or ever played an instrument. As the youngest child, I wanted to stand out from the others. I loved music and had a talent for it. So I took up the saxophone. Music made me unique in my family. That meant a lot to me."

THE SOUND GRABS YOU

Another common reason why people choose the sax is simply because sax music appeals to them. That was the case for sax player Aaron Cohen. "I heard a jazz great on a CD," remembered Cohen. "It grabbed me. I was amazed that

The saxophone could help you stand out. Just don't use it to annoy your sister.

someone could get that kind of sound out of an instrument. It made me want to do the same thing."

Saxophonist Gary Keller had the same experience. "I didn't come from a musical family," Keller said. "But I saw saxophonists on TV when I was young. I heard them on the radio too. I especially liked the great sax solos. I knew that I wanted to play the saxophone. I was in the fifth grade when I had a chance to learn to play an instrument at school. I was really lucky. When it was time to pick our instruments, I got my first choice. It was the sax, of course."

MEET THE CLARINET

Have you ever thought about playing the clarinet? Many sax players were clarinet players first. The sax and the clarinet are both reed instruments. Their sounds are produced in much the same way. If you really like classical music, you may want to give the clarinet a try. It has a soft tone that makes it perfect for classical music.

ALL IN THE FAMILY

Sometimes people just feel drawn to an instrument. They may not know why. That's how it was for sax player Perry Hornkohl. "I always wanted to play tenor sax," Hornkohl said. "I wanted to play it even before I knew the instrument's name. Now I think I know why I was so drawn to it. I was adopted as a young child. Only years later did I learn that my [birth] father was a saxophone player. I think I became a musician because it's in my blood."

The sax is a family tradition for this father and son.

Sax player Sonny Burnette also felt drawn to the saxophone's sound. And like Keller, he first learned to play the saxophone at school. "I had a chance to play in the school band," Burnette recalled. "My other favorite instrument was the bagpipes. As you might have guessed, that instrument wasn't offered. But a used tenor sax was available. I was a tall kid, and it was perfect for me. Now my sax is a part of who I am. It has some nicks and scratches, but those just remind me of what we've been through together."

GOTTA LOVE IT!

Like Keller and Burnette, lots of kids first start playing sax when they enter a school band program. But not every kid sticks with it. Learning to play the sax takes a lot of time, dedication, and hard work.

So what makes some people go on while others quit? Those who keep playing love the saxophone's smooth tones. They love the look and feel of the instrument too. But most of all, they love the music they can make with it. That's the best reason to learn to play any instrument.

CHAPTER FOUR

WHAT DO YOU NEED TO PLAY THE SAXOPHONE?

First, there was the Easter Bunny. Then came the Tooth Fairy and the Happy Birthday Chicken. What if there was a Saxophone Genie? He'd grant kids one musical wish. What would your wish be? Would you want him to snap his fingers and make you a super sax player?

That would be great. But we all know there's no Saxophone Genie. You may have your doubts about

Practice doesn't have to be a chore. You can use the time to show family members what you're learning.

the Happy Birthday Chicken too. That doesn't mean you can't be a great sax player, though. Just be sure to spend your time playing the saxophone, not making wishes.

PRACTICE, PRACTICE, PRACTICE

Practice is the key to success in music. Some people think it's even more important than talent. In college, serious music students may practice five to six hours a day. But don't panic. You don't have to do that now. Sax player Tom McCormick described a good approach for newbies:

"Young beginners can't play for very long at first. Their mouths are going to hurt. They have to get used to blowing on that reed. They can start out practicing about twenty minutes a day. From there, they can work up to a half hour. In time, they can make that an hour. Then they should be in good shape."

Try to practice every day. This will help you to develop the muscles needed to play the sax. It also helps you to become a better musician. Practicing a half hour daily is better than practicing for three hours on the day of your lesson.

BE A PEOPLE PERSON

Musical skills matter. But you need more than that to succeed in the music world. You need people skills too. After all, most of the time, you'll be playing with other musicians.

A few simple rules will help you along the way. Be on time for your practice sessions. Know your part really well. Listen to what the musicians you play with have to say. Their feelings and opinions matter too. Most important, don't demand star treatment for yourself. If you do, your star isn't going to shine too brightly. A lot of people won't want to work with you. Sax player James Noyes summed it up: "Music teaches us how to listen and how to make friends. There are no greater skills in life than these."

The sax players in this Italian brass band work together to make beautiful music.

IT WON'T HAPPEN INSTANTLY

Don't expect a musical miracle. You're not going to sound like a jazz great in a week. It may be a while before you get to where you want to be.

"It takes a long time to sound the way you want to sound on a woodwind instrument," said sax player Stephen Haley. "It doesn't happen overnight. This can be hard for kids who are used to mastering video games in a matter of hours. There are no cheat codes for playing woodwinds. It's not *Guitar Hero*. You have to really want to play well in order to play well."

NO ONE IS PERFECT— ALL THE TIME

Before long, you'll be performing for an audience. You'll want to give a perfect performance every time. Don't count on it, though. Even if you do your best, at times things can go wrong. Instruments have broken during shows. Musicians have slipped onstage. Some have even fallen off the stage.

Some mishaps are out of your control. Others you can take steps to avoid. Knowing your music really well is a big help before going onstage. Sax player Stephen Haley put it this way. "The more you practice for a performance, the more prepared you'll be. If you're not prepared, look out. You can get that 'deer in the headlights' feeling and panic."

It's normal to be nervous before playing for an audience.

"The easiest way to lose your focus is to not be prepared," added sax player Juliene Purefoy. "You've got to really be sure of the music you're about to play. (Not knowing the material) accounts for about 90 percent of what goes wrong during a performance."

OOPS! THERE GOES MY HORN!

Instruments can break during performances. Some musicians always bring a spare sax with them. But most kids have only one instrument. So that may not work for new sax players. Instead, try to get "saxophone smart." Learn to do simple and quick repairs on your instrument.

"Make sure you have your own repair kit handy," advised sax player Joe Donato. "Bring reeds, a small screwdriver, rubber bands, felt, cork, and glue with you. Learn how to use all these things in case you need to."

MEET THE BASSOON

Does a big instrument with a deep sound appeal to you? If so, the bassoon is sure to make you smile. The bassoon is the largest woodwind instrument. It also has the lowest pitch.

Bassoons vary in length from 5 to 8 feet (1.5 to 2.4 meters). Even a 5-foot bassoon would be too big to play if it were stretched out to its full length. So the instrument is doubled back on itself. That way, players can cover all the keys with their fingers.

The bassoon has a special job in orchestras. It's often used for funny moments in musical pieces. That's why it's sometimes called the clown of the orchestra.

The bassoon is a large instrument, even for a grown-up.

Sax player Sonny Burnette once needed to do some emergency repairs on his sax moments before a performance. "I was getting ready to perform when it happened," he said. "It was so cold outside the performance space that my sax's metal contracted (shrank). The glue holding one pad in place cracked, and the pad fell out. I had to quickly re-glue the pad. It's best to always be prepared and to expect the unexpected!"

Mishaps can happen to anyone. What matters is how you handle them. Try to take things in stride. Don't panic onstage. Do your best to continue performing—no matter what.

CREATIVITY WORKS

Sax players are creative. You can hear it in their music. Let that creativity work for you in other ways too. At times,

Playing the sax gives you plenty of chances to be creative.

A COMMON BOND

According to sax player Gary Keller, getting together with other musicians is one of the best parts of playing music. "I like being around other musicians," Keller said. "They're my kind of people. The music unites us. We share a common bond. It starts when you're in school and gets stronger your whole life."

it can save a performance. That was the case for sax player James Noyes. Here's how he solved a problem and saved the day. "Once I forgot to bring my neck strap to a performance. I needed that strap to hold the sax around my neck. I had to make a neck strap out of something. The only thing available was a wire coat hanger. I bent the wire hanger around my neck and through the hook on the sax. It was quite uncomfortable, but it did the trick that day. As they say, the show must go on!"

Loving your saxophone and your music is a great first step toward sharing music with others. And if something goes wrong, the audience can be more understanding than you might think. In time you'll get where you want to be. Your listeners will love you and the music you play for them.

QUIZ: IS THE SAXOPHONE RIGHT FOR YOU?

Which of these statements describes you best? Please record your answers on a separate sheet of paper.

1. If at first you don't succeed,
- **A.** You try, try again. You like to finish what you start. People say you're the determined type.
- **B.** You feel that a lack of success means it wasn't meant to be. You prefer to try something else you may be better at.

2. When you hear a good piece of music,
- **A.** You get really into all the sounds. You feel as if you could listen to the piece forever!
- **B.** You think it sounds good, but you don't usually get too absorbed in it. You'd rather spend time working on art or learning new soccer moves than listening closely to music.

3. When you're doing a task that requires fine motor skills,
- **A.** Your fingers are quick and nimble. Detailed tasks are fun for you.
- **B.** You tend to drop things or get frustrated. Taking bike rides or playing video games is more up your alley than working with your hands.

4. When you're working toward a long-term goal,
- **A.** You tend to be patient. Practicing a skill again and again doesn't bother you.
- **B.** You get a little antsy. You'd rather move on to something new than focus on the same task for a long time.

5. When you think about practicing your instrument,
- **A.** You get really excited. You think studying an instrument sounds like fun!
- **B.** You like music, but you can think of other things you'd rather do. Giving up free time to practice every day doesn't sound worth it.

Were your answers mostly A's?

If so, the saxophone may just be the right choice for you!

GLOSSARY

bell: the bell-shaped end of the saxophone

bow: the U-shaped bottom of the saxophone's body

ensemble: a small musical group

improvisation: making up parts of the music you play while you are playing it

key: a button that a sax player presses to play a specific note

neck: a curved tube attached to the saxophone's body

pitch: the highness or lowness of a sound

reed: a slim piece of wood that is attached to the saxophone's mouthpiece

solo: a musical performance in which a performer plays alone

thumb rest: a hook-shaped part on the saxophone used to support the sax's weight

tube: the straight part of the saxophone's body

woodwind family: a group of instruments that produce sound when air is blown over or through them

SOURCE NOTES

7   James Hayward, e-mail message to author, August 6, 2009.

22–23   James Noyes, telephone conversation with author, September 20, 2009.

23   George Garzone, telephone conversation with author, September 29, 2009.

24   Kermit Virgil, interview with author, May 26, 2009.

24–25   Aaron Cohen, interview with author, July 8, 2009.

25   Gary Keller, interview with author, June 3, 2009.

26   Perry Hornkohl, telephone conversation with author, July 29, 2009.

27   Sonny Burnette, e-mail message to author, July 28, 2009.

29   Tom McCormick, interview with author, June 5, 2009.

31   Stephen Haley, e-mail message to author, September 24, 2009.

31   Ibid.

32   Juliene Purefoy, interview with author, August 6, 2009.

32   Joe Donato, e-mail message to author, August 22, 2009.

34   Burnette.

35   Keller.

35   Noyes.

SELECTED BIBLIOGRAPHY

Ingham, Richard. *The Cambridge Companion to the Saxophone.* New York: Cambridge University Press, 1998.

Morales, Ed. *Latin Beat: The Rhythm and Roots of Latin Music from Bossa Nova to Salsa and Beyond.* Cambridge, MA: Da Capo Press, 2003.

Priestley, Brian. *Chasin' the Bird: The Life and Legacy of Charlie Parker.* New York: Oxford University Press, 2006.

FOR MORE INFORMATION

Dallas Symphony Orchestra: Kids
http://www.dsokids.com
Visit this website to learn about the saxophone and listen to the sounds it makes. Don't miss the link to fun music-related games!

Kenney, Karen Latchana. *Cool Rock Music: Create and Appreciate What Makes Music Great!* Edina, MN: Abdo, 2008. This book introduces rock music and the instruments used to play it. There's also information on writing a rock song and making a rock video.

Landau, Elaine. *Is the Guitar for You?* Minneapolis: Lerner Publications Company, 2011. If the saxophone isn't right for you, check out the guitar. This book covers guitar basics, including what the instrument looks like and what music it is used to play.

PBS Kids Go!: Jazz Greats
Check out this website to learn more about Charlie Parker and others.
http://pbskids.org/jazz/nowthen/index.html

THE SAXOPHONISTS WHO HELPED WITH THIS BOOK

This book could not have been written without the insights of these saxophonists.

SONNY BURNETTE
Sonny Burnette is the chair of the music department at Georgetown College in Georgetown, Kentucky.

AARON COHEN
Aaron Cohen plays with the jazz group the Aaron Cohen Trio.

JOE DONATO
Joe Donato has performed with Cher, Roberta Flack, and Art Blakey.

GEORGE GARZONE
George Garzone is a member of the jazz trio the Fringe. He's also a jazz educator.

STEPHEN HALEY
Stephen Haley has been an instrumentalist, a bandleader, and a teacher.

JAMES HAYWARD
James Hayward plays with the Palm Beach Pops in South Florida.

PERRY HORNKOHL
Perry Hornkohl is a music educator and plays all styles of music.

GARY KELLER
Gary Keller is with the University of Miami Studio Music and Jazz program.

TOM MCCORMICK
Tom McCormick is on the faculty of Miami-Dade College and the New World School of the Arts.

JAMES NOYES
James Noyes is a teacher, a scholar, and a composer.

JULIENE PUREFOY
Juliene Purefoy is a composer, arranger, and music educator.

KERMIT VIRGIL
Kermit Virgil is the director of bands at Booker T. Washington High School in Miami.

INDEX

PHOTO ACKNOWLEDGMENTS

The images in this book are used with the permission of: © Macromayer/dreamstime.com, p. 1; © iStockphoto.com/Graham Yuile, p. 3; © Leland Bobbe/Getty Images, p. 4; © photographer/SuperStock, p. 5; © Karlene Schwartz, pp. 6, 10, 25, 33; © Csocci/ Dreamstime.com, p. 7; © Digital Vision/Getty Images, p. 8; © age fotostock/SuperStock, p. 9; AP Photo/Alex Brandon, p. 11; © iStockphoto.com/Michael Fernahl, pp. 12-13; © Catherine McGann/Contributor/Getty Images, p. 14; AP Photo/Taya Lynn Gray, p. 15; AP Photo/Christof Stache, p. 16; © 2005 Getty Images, pp. 17, 19; © James Quine/Alamy, p. 18; © Lonely Planet/ SuperStock, pp. 20, 30; AP Photo/Ron Edmonds, p. 21; © Jupiter Images/Getty Images, p. 22; © Aizar Raldes/AFP/Getty Images, p. 23; © Steve Satushek/Getty Images, p. 24; © Jeff Cadge/Getty Images, p. 26; © Ableimages/Getty Images, p. 27; © Simon Jarratt/CORBIS, p. 28; © Scott Montgomery/Getty Images, p. 32; © Jose Luis Pelaez Inc./Getty Images, p. 34.

Front cover: © Marcomayer/Dreamstime.com.